BEYOND THE Rx

PENDOWN PRESS LLP

An ISO 9001 & ISO 14001 Certified Co.,

Regd. Office: 3767A, Kanhaiya Nagar,
Tri Nagar, Delhi-110035
Ph.: 8130886000, 9650072927
E-mail: info@pendownpress.com
Branch Office: 1A/2A, 20, Hari Sadan, Ansari Road,
Daryaganj, New Delhi-110002
Ph.: 011-45794768
Website: PendownPress.com

Edition: 2025
Price: ₹ 399
ISBN: 978-93-6338-975-5

Layout and Cover Designed by Pendown Graphics Team
Printed and Bound in India by Thomson Press India Ltd.

In loving memory of my father
(Bharat bhai) –
Your absence is felt deeply, yet your
guidance echoes in every decision I make.
This book is a tribute to the strong
foundation you laid in my life.

CONTENTS

Part 3: Communicate - The Doctor-Patient Connection

Part 4: Empower - Your Staff, Your Secret Weapon

Case Studies: Real Clinics, Real Results

Conclusion: Your Patient-First Practice: A Thriving Future

PREFACE

Dear Reader,

This book is not a lecture, not a course, and definitely not a magic trick. It is just a heartfelt effort. A collection of thoughts, experiences, and simple suggestions that I believe can truly help.

Over the years, I have met many doctors who are excellent at what they do. Yet somewhere in the busyness of daily practice, the small things get missed. Things that could make a big difference in the way patients feel, respond, and return.

This book is written with full respect for the medical profession and with the belief that even small efforts like a smile at the front desk, a follow-up message, or a clean chair in the waiting room can go a long way in creating trust and loyalty.

I am not here to teach. I am here to share.

If even one page of this book helps you improve your patient's experience and makes your day at the clinic a little smoother and a little happier, then this effort was worth it.

Thank you for giving your time to this.

Let us begin this journey with an open mind and a simple goal. To make things just a little better, one step at a time.

Warm regards,

Neerav Shah

ACKNOWLEDGEMENTS

Every milestone I've reached, every step forward, none of it would have been possible without the people who stood beside me, quietly and unconditionally.

To My Father

If I've ever flown, it's only because you gave me wings. Your values, quiet trust, and constant belief shaped who I am. I keenly feel your absence, yet I know you are always watching over me, a constant source of guidance and inspiration.

To My Family

To my pillars of strength — my mother, sister, wife and children

You are the quiet strength behind every step I've taken, the foundation of everything I am and everything I aspire to be.

Your love has never asked for recognition, yet it has carried me through every chapter of my life. In your quiet strength, I've found stability; in your unwavering belief, I've found the courage to dream; and in your constant presence, I've found peace amidst life's chaos. Whether it was through a prayer said in silence, a word of encouragement at the right moment, or the warmth of shared laughter during the hardest days, you've been there, steady and strong.

You've held me up when I felt weak, reminded me of my purpose when I was lost, and celebrated my smallest victories as if they were your own. Through every joy and every struggle, you've shown me that family isn't just who we're born to, it's the circle that protects, uplifts, and never lets go.

This book is a reflection of all you've poured into me, your faith, your patience, your love. It belongs as much to you as it does to me.

To My Mentors

Your wisdom has been a guiding light throughout my journey.

Thank you for generously sharing your time, insights, and belief in me.

Your influence has shaped not just my work, but the way I think, lead, and grow.

To My Team

You are the heartbeat behind every achievement.

Your passion, dedication, and relentless pursuit of excellence have turned ideas into impactful realities.

I'm deeply grateful to walk this journey with people who believe in the vision and bring it to life with such energy and heart.

To The Doctors

To the doctors I've had the privilege of meeting and learning from, your trust, time, and openness have meant the world.

Regularly visiting your clinics, listening to your feedback, and exchanging ideas has been a transformative part of this journey.

Your insights, challenges, and stories have opened new doors for learning and growth, and they have played a key role in shaping the clarity, direction, and depth of this book.

Thank you for being both inspiration and compassion in this mission.

To Mr. Dinesh Verma and the Entire Pendown Press Team

This book wouldn't exist without your commitment, creativity, and care. Thank you for bringing it to life.

And lastly, to every friend, family member and well-wisher whether named or unnamed, your presence in my life is a blessing.

This journey is bigger than me.

It belongs to all of us.

Thank you from the bottom of my heart.

AUTHOR'S CORNER

I didn't inherit a company. I inherited a mindset.

A mindset shaped by my father's discipline, curiosity and willingness to dive deep into an industry that was once unfamiliar to him but quickly became his life's passion.

Hello, my name is Neerav and I am a second-generation entrepreneur in the pharmaceutical industry. My father was a passionate businessman and a pioneer in the generic wholesale business in Kolkata. He was an incredibly hard-working man, dedicating 16-18 hours each day to his work. For him, it wasn't merely about financial success; the pharmaceutical business had become his true calling. Despite coming from a different educational background, his knowledge and expertise rivaled those of any doctor or pharmacist. He had an instinctive understanding of medicine and healing, something that can't be taught, only lived. Ultimately, his passion drove him to establish a pharmaceutical manufacturing facility for oral dosage forms, laying the foundation for what would become a lifelong journey for both of us.

As his son, I inherited his entrepreneurial spirit. Witnessing his dedication and passion ignited my own interest in medicine. Although my academic background lay elsewhere, I eventually joined him. In 2005, I fully committed myself to the family business of pharmaceutical marketing and manufacturing. I've never looked back.

Over time, I became captivated by every dimension of this field; how medicines are manufactured and tested, how they are released into the market, how physicians prescribe them, how distributors and retailers sell them, how patients acquire them, how they interact within the body, how they work pharmacologically, how they eradicate disease, and how patients ultimately recover.

This science deeply intrigued me not just for its technical complexity but for its human impact. Behind every tablet lies a story of research, regulation, trust and hope. And I resolved to dedicate my life to it.

Beyond our own manufacturing operations, I built strong relationships with numerous colleagues in the industry. We initiated "P2P (Principle To Principle)" manufacturing agreements to accelerate market penetration for our products within the dynamic Indian pharmaceutical landscape. The Indian pharmaceutical market stands as one of the largest globally, defined by its extensive range of products, vast patient base, and a multitude of competing companies.

Throughout my business activities, I have traveled extensively, visiting countless doctors. I observed that approx 95% of physicians do not engage in any form of marketing to retain their patients. Instead, many lament declining market conditions or a perceived lack of patients. In India, it has become commonplace for doctors to avoid self-promotion, a trend which, in my view, represents a significant misstep.

What I came to realize is this: regardless of whether you are a banker, lawyer, or doctor, marketing serves as the backbone of sustainability. If you fail to effectively communicate your expertise to your clients, you will inevitably be replaced. **Competence is vital but visibility is survival.**

My two decades of experience in pharmaceutical marketing have provided invaluable insights into how a physician can maintain a thriving practice and how patients can develop a strong affinity for their doctor. The strategies outlined in this book are both ethical and easily implementable. The only requirement is a willingness to embrace a new mindset and apply these strategies consistently.

This book is a sincere attempt to bridge the gap between great medical service and effective communication. It's time that doctors take charge not just of their clinical practice but of their presence, perception, and patient relationships.

INTRODUCTION

INDIAN PHARMA: FROM MOLECULES TO MEANINGFUL PATIENT CARE

> ***"Share what you know. Your patients will repay you a hundredfold."***

For context, projections indicate that the Indian pharmaceutical market will reach a valuation of approximately ₹2.38 lakh crore by 2025 (data sourced from reputable news publications). According to the National Medical Commission (NMC), as of June 2022, India had **1.38 million registered allopathic physicians** and **565,000 AYUSH practitioners**. While the World Health Organization (WHO) recommends a doctor-to-patient ratio of 1:1000, India currently stands at **1:834**, exceeding that benchmark.

This raises a critical and often overlooked question:

Out of these 1.38 million doctors, how many actively and ethically market their services to build a meaningful, thriving practice? How many go beyond clinical treatment to build real, lasting relationships with patients, relationships that go both ways?

In my 20 years of meeting physicians, I have rarely come across instances where doctors proactively send even a simple *"How are you?"* message or make follow-up calls to their patients after treatment.

There is a prevailing assumption in our country that once a

patient departs a physician's office, they will diligently take their prescribed medication and ultimately recover. However, in reality, patients often feel forgotten. Rarely do they follow up with updates or express gratitude not because they don't care, but because no one initiated the conversation.

India, with its diverse geography and vast population, experiences a wide spectrum of climatic conditions and varying patterns of epidemics, infections, and diseases. Typically, patient footfall decreases significantly during periods of extreme heat (around 42 degrees Celsius) or extreme cold (around 10 degrees Celsius or below). Conversely, during the transitional seasons (summer to winter, winter to summer) or after periods of rainfall, physician offices experience a surge in patient volume.

During periods of lower patient volume, physicians frequently voice concerns about a lack of business. Yet, when patient numbers increase, these same physicians are generally content. Therefore, if asked what a doctor does to proactively increase patient volume, my honest response would be nothing – they simply rely on seasonal fluctuations.

But times have changed. Today's world demands more than just medical excellence. Doctors must recognize that modern medical practice requires marketing. Physicians who adopt a patient-centric approach will thrive, resulting in favorable outcomes for both the practitioner and those they serve. The strategies I will explore in the following chapters are grounded in ethical and legal principles. Upon reading this book, I am confident that members of the medical community will not only agree with my perspectives but also wish they had implemented these simple strategies sooner.

What This Book Will Add to Your Practice (and Your Patients' Lives)

So, let's not wait anymore and begin this journey of transformation.

Part 1 starts now!

PART 1

CONNECT

THE KEEP-IN-TOUCH TOOLKIT

Why Most Doctors Miss This Simple Trick: The Power of "Keep-In-Touch"

Let's be honest, doctors. Most of you are very busy. Between long hours, back-to-back patients, emergency calls, and endless paperwork, your focus naturally stays on diagnosing and treating illnesses. And that's truly admirable.

But there's one simple, often overlooked strategy that can dramatically improve your practice: **Keeping in touch with your patients.**

The truth is, the vast majority of doctors in smaller cities and towns don't actively stay in touch with their patients after they leave the clinic. They rely solely on patients remembering their next appointment or returning when they feel sick again. This passive approach misses a major opportunity to:

- Build deeper relationships
- Improve treatment adherence and outcomes
- Strengthen patient loyalty
- Grow a more resilient and respected practice

Think about it:

A simple, well-timed message, whether it's a prescription reminder, a follow-up on recovery, or a festival greeting can make a patient feel genuinely valued. And the best part? When it's sent in their local language: Hindi, Bengali, or whichever dialect your patients relate to, it becomes more than just a message. It becomes a connection. This personal touch makes all the difference.

In this section, we'll explore simple "Keep-In-Touch" (KIT) strategies that you can easily implement to connect with your patients on a deeper level. These are proven methods for building loyalty, improving health outcomes, and creating a thriving practice – all without spending a fortune or becoming a tech expert. Are you ready to unlock the power of "Keep-In-Touch"?

Let's begin building a practice where patients feel seen, supported and always connected.

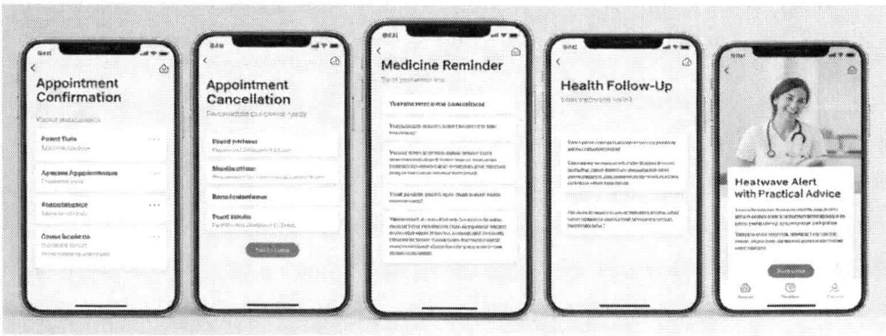

KIT Essentials: *SMS/WhatsApp Templates That Work*

"The best medicine often starts with a message."

Remember, all messages should be translated into the local language (Hindi, Bengali, etc.)

1. **Pre-Visit KIT: Making Appointments Easy and Reliable**
   - **Summary:** These messages ensure patients don't forget appointments and encourage timely cancellations, improving time management for both doctor and patient.
   - **Example 1: Appointment Confirmation with Added Value**
     - **Message:** "Dear [Patient Name], your appointment with Dr. [Your Name] is confirmed for [Date] at

[Time]. Please arrive 15 minutes early to complete paperwork. If you have any questions, call us at [Phone Number]."

  - **Patient Reaction:** "Great, thanks for the reminder! I appreciate knowing I need to arrive early for paperwork; it helps me plan my day."

- **Example 2: Appointment Cancellation Reminder (with Emphasis on Helping Others)**
  - **Message:** "Dear [Patient Name], we understand things come up. If you can't make your appointment on [Date] at [Time], please let us know at least 2 hours in advance so another patient can see the doctor sooner. Call [Phone Number] to reschedule."
  - **Patient Reaction:** "I appreciate the reminder and the understanding. I'll definitely call if I can't make it; it's good to know I'd be helping someone else."

2. **Post-Visit KIT: Continuing Care Beyond the Consultation Room**

- **Summary:** These messages demonstrate ongoing care and support, boosting patient compliance and overall well-being.
- **Example 1: Medicine Reminder with Important Instructions**
  - **Message:** "Dear [Patient Name], a reminder from Dr. [Your Name] to take your [Medicine Name] as prescribed: [Dosage] [Frequency] [With/Without Food]. Call us at [Phone Number] if you have any questions or side effects."
  - **Patient Reaction:** "This is so helpful! I always forget whether to take that medicine with food. Now I have it in writing."

- **Example 2: Health Follow-Up with a Personal Touch**
    - **Message:** "Dear [Patient Name], Dr. [Your Name] hopes you're feeling better since your visit on [Date]. Please remember to [Specific Recommendation from Visit]. If you have any concerns, don't hesitate to call."
    - **Patient Reaction:** "It's thoughtful that they remembered my specific recommendation! It shows they really paid attention during my visit."

3. **Awareness KIT: Empowering Patients with Knowledge**
    - **Summary:** These messages provide timely and relevant health information, empowering patients to take proactive steps for their well-being.
    - **Example 1: Monsoon Precautions with Specific Actions**
        - **Message:** "Protect yourself and your family from dengue this monsoon season! Use mosquito repellent, wear long sleeves, and remove standing water around your home. Visit our clinic if you experience fever, headache, or body aches."
        - **Patient Reaction:** "That's a helpful reminder! I'll make sure to empty those flower pots in my yard."
    - **Example 2: Heatwave Alert with Practical Advice**
        - **Message:** "A heatwave is predicted this week! Stay indoors during peak hours (11 AM - 4 PM), drink plenty of fluids, and wear light-colored, loose-fitting clothing. Seek medical attention immediately if you experience dizziness, nausea, or confusion."

  - **Patient Reaction:** "I didn't realize the heatwave was going to be that bad. I'll definitely stay inside during the hottest part of the day."

4. **Greetings KIT: Celebrating Milestones and Building Connections**
   - **Summary:** These messages add a personal touch, making patients feel valued and appreciated beyond their medical needs.
   - **Example 1: Birthday Wish with a Health Focus**
     - **Message:** "Dear [Patient Name], Happy Birthday from Dr. [Your Name] and our entire team! We wish you a year filled with good health, happiness, and well-being. Don't forget to schedule your annual check-up!"
     - **Patient Reaction:** "That's such a nice birthday message! And it reminded me I'm due for a check-up – smart and thoughtful!"
   - **Example 2: Anniversary Wish with a Personal Touch**
     - **Message:** "Dear [Patient Name], Happy Anniversary! Dr. [Your Name] and our team wish you both many more years of happiness and good health together. We appreciate you choosing us for your care."
     - **Patient Reaction:** "That's so sweet and unexpected! It really makes me feel like they care about me as a person, not just a patient."

I believe these longer, more detailed messages strike a good balance between providing valuable information and building a meaningful personal connection with patients.

Automate Your Communication: *Set It and (Almost) Forget It*

"You heal faster when your hands are free from the keyboard."

Let's be real, Doctor. You're already working long hours. You don't have time to become a messaging expert or spend hours every week manually sending reminders to your patients. That's why **automation** is the key to making the "Keep-In-Touch" *system works for you, not against you.*

If you're thinking, "Automation? That sounds complicated!", relax. It's simpler than you think. The goal is to **find a system that lets you send messages to multiple patients at once**, without having to type each message individually. We want to free you from the technicalities so you can focus on what you do best: taking care of patients.

Why Automation is a Must:

- **Saves You Time:** This is the biggest benefit. Automation frees up your valuable time so you can focus on patient care, not tedious administrative tasks.
- **Ensures Consistency:** Automated systems ensure that messages are sent reliably and consistently, every time. You won't have to worry about forgetting to send a reminder or follow-up message.
- **Reduces Errors:** Manual data entry is prone to errors. Automated systems minimize the risk of sending incorrect or incomplete information to your patients.

- **Scalable:** As your practice grows, an automated system can easily handle the increased volume of messages without requiring you to hire additional staff.
- **Reduces Burden:** You should not feel that sending a message is a burden on your daily activities.

How to Automate: Simple Options for Busy Doctors

The good news!!! You don't need expensive software or tech skills. Below are three practical automation approaches from low-tech to more advanced, so you can start wherever you're most comfortable.

1. **The "Helper" Method (Low-Tech, but Effective):**
   - Find a trustworthy person (a family member, a college student, or a reliable member of your community, or your assistant) who is comfortable with technology. This could be a person who has experience with a computer or has the willingness to learn.
   - Create a spreadsheet (using Excel or Google Sheets) with your patient names, phone numbers, and appointment dates.
   - Provide them with the message templates (translated into the local language, of course!).
   - Train them to use a free online SMS service to send the messages to your patients.

   Benefits: This method is simple, affordable, and doesn't require any technical expertise on your part.

   Drawbacks: It relies on a human being, so there's a risk of errors. Make sure you select the right person, the one who you can trust.

2. **The Spreadsheet + Bulk SMS Method (A Step Up):**
   - This method is similar to the "Helper" method, but you take on a little more of the responsibility yourself.
   - You create and maintain the patient spreadsheet.
   - You use a "bulk SMS" service to send the messages. Many of these services offer free trials or very affordable rates.

   Benefits: More control over the messaging process. Can be more cost-effective than hiring a helper in the long run.

   Drawbacks: Requires a little more technical knowledge (using spreadsheets and online SMS services).

3. **Clinic Management Software (The Most Efficient Option):**
   - Many clinic management software programs now include built-in SMS messaging features.
   - These programs integrate directly with your patient database and allow you to send automated reminders and follow-up messages with just a few clicks.

   Benefits: Seamless integration with your existing workflow. Streamlined communication. More advanced features (e.g., personalized messages, appointment scheduling).

   Drawbacks: Can be more expensive than the other options. May require some training to use the software effectively.

The Bottom Line

The key is to choose a method that works for you and your practice's current stage. Don't let the fear of technology hold you back. Even the simplest automation can save hours, reduce stress, and strengthen your patient relationships.

Start with a simple system, and gradually upgrade as your needs evolve. The effort you put into automating your communication will pay off in the long run with more loyal patients, improved health outcomes, and a less stressful work life.

Patient Loyalty on Autopilot: *Building Relationships That Last a Lifetime*

"Connection is the cure that doesn't need a prescription."

Let's talk about something even more valuable than a full waiting room, Doctors: **Patient loyalty**. It's the bedrock of a thriving practice, the key to long-term success, and the foundation of a truly fulfilling career.

Think about it: wouldn't you rather have a practice filled with patients who trust you, value your advice, and recommend you to their friends and family? Of course, you would! And that's exactly what "Keep-In-Touch" (KIT) strategies can help you achieve.

It's not just about filling appointment slots; it's about building lasting relationships with your patients. It's about becoming a trusted figure in their lives, someone they rely on for their health needs, year after year.

Why Patient Loyalty Matters (More Than You Think):

- **Consistent Revenue:** Loyal patients keep coming back, providing a steady stream of income for your practice. You spend less time and money attracting new patients and more time focusing on the patients you already have.

- **Reduced Marketing Costs:** Word-of-mouth marketing is the most powerful (and cheapest!) form of advertising. Happy, loyal patients will naturally recommend you to their friends, family, and neighbors.
- **Improved Patient Outcomes:** Patients who trust you are more likely to follow your advice, adhere to their treatment plans, and achieve better health outcomes.
- **Reduced Stress:** When you have a practice full of loyal, appreciative patients, your work life becomes less stressful and more rewarding. You'll spend less time dealing with difficult patients and more time focusing on what you love: providing excellent care.
- **A Fulfilling Career:** The greatest reward of being a doctor isn't just the money; it's the satisfaction of knowing that you're making a positive impact on people's lives. Building long-term relationships with your patients allows you to experience that fulfillment firsthand.

KIT: The Key to Unlocking Lifelong Relationships

So how does "Keep-In-Touch" help you build this kind of lasting loyalty?

It's simple: it shows your patients that you care about them as people, not just as patients. This small shift in approach can change the way your entire practice is perceived.

- **It Shows You Remember Them:** A simple appointment reminder or follow-up message demonstrates that you value their time and their well-being.
- **It Shows You're Proactive About Their Health:** Sending seasonal health tips, vaccination alerts, or medication reminders shows that you're invested in their long-term health.

- **It Shows You Appreciate Them:** A birthday or anniversary greeting adds a personal touch that makes patients feel valued and appreciated. These small gestures go a long way in building emotional loyalty.
- **It Builds Trust:** By consistently communicating with your patients, you establish yourself as a reliable and trustworthy source of information. Regular touchpoints reinforce the idea that you're always there for them, not just during sickness.

The Long-Term Payoff: A Practice Built on Relationships

Think of your practice as a garden. You can't just plant the seeds (treat the illnesses) and then walk away. You need to nurture the soil, water the plants, and provide ongoing care. "Keep-In-Touch" is the fertilizer that helps your practice flourish, creating a vibrant ecosystem of loyal patients who will support you for years to come.

By investing in "Keep-In-Touch" strategies, you're not just filling appointment slots; you're building a legacy of care, trust, and lasting relationships. And that is a reward that's worth more than any amount of money.

Cycle of Automated Patient Loyalty

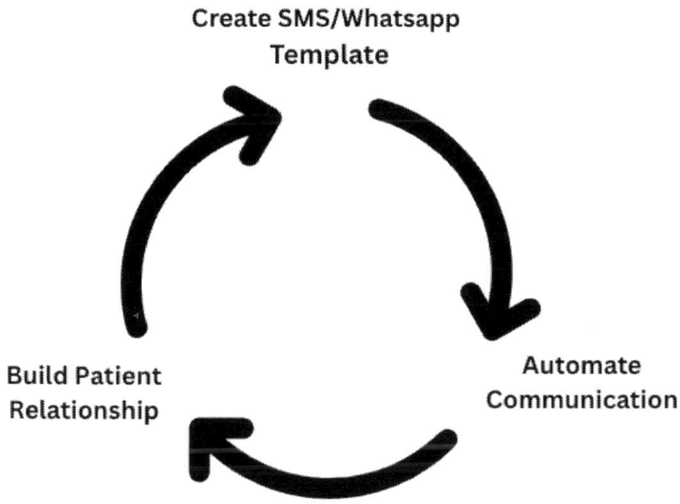

PART 2

Transform
The Waiting Room Revolution

Let's face it, Doctors. For many patients especially in smaller cities and towns, visiting a doctor's office isn't something they look forward to. In fact, often something they dread. And the waiting room, in particular, is usually the biggest source of that discomfort, filled with stress, anxiety, and sometimes even discomfort.

It's not just a holding area before consultation; it's the **first impression zone**. And what patients feel there often shapes how they perceive the entire experience, no matter how good the treatment is.

Before we talk about solutions, let's paint a realistic picture of what a typical waiting room looks like today:

The Current Reality: A Waiting Room Nightmare

Hygiene? What Hygiene?

In many clinics, basic hygiene is often lacking.

- Chairs are often stained and dusty.
- Floors are rarely mopped or swept.
- The air is often stuffy and stale.
- Hand sanitizers are non-existent.

This creates an immediate negative impression and raises concerns about infection control. In today's health-conscious world, a visibly unhygienic space isn't just unpleasant; it feels unsafe.

Patient's silent thought: "If this is how they maintain their clinic, how well will they manage my treatment?"

The Endless Wait: Patients often wait for hours to see the doctor, even with a scheduled appointment. This is due to overbooking, inefficient scheduling, and the doctor's own busy schedule.

Lack of Basic Amenities

Many waiting rooms lack even the most basic amenities.

- There's often no clean drinking water available.
- Restrooms are often dirty and ill-equipped.
- There's no air conditioning or fans, making the wait unbearable during hot weather.

Value addition: These are not luxuries; they're patient rights. Imagine a mother with a toddler, or an elderly patient needing to hydrate or use the restroom, these things matter.

Crowded and Chaotic

Waiting rooms are often overcrowded, with patients crammed into a small space. This creates a sense of chaos and anxiety. There's often no privacy, with patients overhearing each other's conversations, there is often no system to monitor the patients.

Patient's experience: "Why are people going in before me?" Without a visible queue or token system, confusion breeds irritation.

Boredom and Frustration

With long wait times and no distractions, patients often become bored and frustrated. They're left staring at the walls, feeling ignored and unimportant.

Simple improvement: A TV screen playing health tips, patient success stories, or even light instrumental music can shift the mood. Magazines or informative posters also help patients feel mentally engaged, not abandoned.

The Impact of a Bad Waiting Room Experience

This negative waiting room experience has a significant impact on your patients:

- **Increased Anxiety:** The uncomfortable environment and long wait times can trigger anxiety and stress, especially for patients who are already worried about their health.
- **Decreased Satisfaction:** Patients are less likely to be satisfied with their overall experience, even if the doctor provides excellent medical care.
- **Loss of Trust:** A dirty, disorganized waiting room can erode patients' trust in the doctor's competence and professionalism.
- **Reduced Loyalty:** Unhappy patients are less likely to return to your clinic and more likely to seek care elsewhere.
- **Damage to Your Reputation:** Negative word-of-mouth can spread quickly, damaging your clinic's reputation and making it harder to attract new patients.

But here's the good news, Doctor: It doesn't have to be this way! With just a few simple changes, you can transform your waiting room from a source of stress and anxiety into a welcoming and comfortable space that enhances the patient experience.

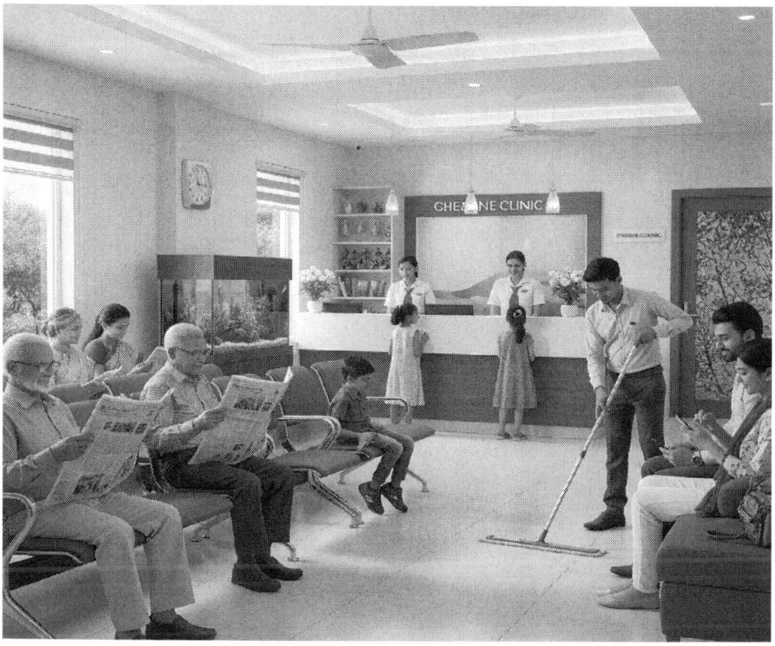

The 5-Minute Hygiene Checklist: Quick & Easy

> ***"The cleaner your clinic feels, the louder your care is heard."***

Even if you're short on time and staff, these five small actions can instantly make your waiting room look more professional, more inviting—and more trusted. They're quick, budget-friendly, and highly effective.

1. **Surface Scan:** Quickly wipe down all chairs, tables, and door handles with a disinfectant wipe. A single wipe costs pennies, but the peace of mind it gives patients is priceless.

2. **Air Quality:** Open windows to air out the room and spray a quick burst of air freshener. Fresh air is free, and a pleasant scent can make a world of difference. It turns "stuffy and stale" into "calm and clean" within seconds.
3. **Hand Sanitizer Station:** Ensure a bottle of hand sanitizer is readily available and visible. Patients may not ask for it, but they'll notice if it's missing. Bonus points if you include a small printed sign that encourages use.
4. **Reading Material Refresh:** Remove any old, torn, or dusty magazines and replace them with a few clean newspapers or newer publications. Even better: swap them occasionally with health tips or simple preventive care posters. It shows you're not just treating illness, you're promoting wellness.
5. **Floor Check:** Do a quick sweep or mop to remove any visible dirt or debris.

The Impact

These simple actions take just a few minutes each day but create a significant improvement in the overall cleanliness and hygiene of your waiting room. Patients will notice the difference and appreciate your attention to detail.

Creating Calm: Simple Ways to Reduce Patient Anxiety

"An uncluttered space quiets the cluttered mind."

A waiting room should be a place where patients can relax and feel at ease, not a source of stress and anxiety. For many patients, especially those already worried about their health, the environment plays a crucial role in shaping their mindset even before they see the doctor.

Here are some simple ways to create a more calming environment:

1. **Lighting:** Replace harsh fluorescent lights with softer, warmer lighting.

   Why it matters: Harsh lights can increase stress and make the space feel clinical or cold. Warmer lighting creates a more inviting, homely atmosphere that puts patients at ease the moment they walk in.

2. **Music:** Play soothing instrumental music at a low volume. Avoid loud, jarring music or talk radio.

   Bonus tip: Classical piano, soft flute, or natural sounds are known to lower blood pressure and reduce waiting anxiety especially for elderly patients and children.

3. **Colors:** Use calming colors like blues, greens, and earth tones on the walls and furniture.

   Colors influence emotion. Cool tones (like soft blue or sage green) promote relaxation, while bright reds or yellows can increase tension.

4. **Clutter Control:** Remove any unnecessary clutter from the waiting room. A clean and organized space feels more calming.

   Keep counters tidy, avoid excessive posters or hanging wires, and store files or supplies out of sight. Visual noise adds to mental stress.

5. **Plants:** Add a few plants to the waiting room. Plants add a touch of nature and create a more welcoming environment.

Even a single indoor plant or small potted greenery in a corner can make a space feel more alive, more human. Choose low-maintenance options like snake plants or peace lilies.

The Impact

By creating a more calming environment, you can reduce patient anxiety, increase comfort, and make their waiting experience more pleasant.

Turning Wait Time into Win Time: Engaging Patients Instantly... and Showing You Care

> ***"Make your waiting room your first handshake. It should say, 'You matter here.'"***

Long wait times are inevitable in a busy practice, but you can make the wait more bearable and even demonstrate your care for your patients with these simple additions:

1. **Health Information Posters (in the Local Language!):** Display posters about common health problems in your community, like seasonal illnesses, diabetes, hypertension, or maternal care tips.
2. **Local News:** Provide newspapers or magazines featuring local news and events.
3. **Patient Education Materials:** Offer brochures or pamphlets about common medical conditions, treatments, and preventive care. Consider including QR codes linking to short videos or articles in Hindi or regional languages for those who prefer audio-visual formats.
4. **Comfortable Seating:** Ensure the waiting room has comfortable seating, with enough space for everyone to sit comfortably.

5. **Something for the Little Ones:** Add a small basket of simple, inexpensive toys for children to play with. A few building blocks, a coloring book, or some toy cars can make a huge difference for parents with restless kids.
6. **Essentials for Every Patient:** Offer complimentary masks and a small bottle of hand sanitizer to each patient upon arrival. This shows you prioritize their health and well-being.

The Cost: A Tiny Investment, a Huge Return

Let's be realistic, Doctor. All of these additions cost money. A mask, a small bottle of sanitizer, and a cup of water might cost you, what, ₹20 per patient? It seems insignificant.

But consider what you gain:

- **Increased Patient Satisfaction:** Patients will appreciate your thoughtfulness and attention to detail.
- **Enhanced Trust:** By providing these small comforts, you're building trust and demonstrating that you care about their well-being.
- **Improved Loyalty:** Happy, comfortable patients are more likely to return to your clinic and recommend you to others.

The return on that ₹20 investment is unmeasurable. It's about building a reputation for excellence and creating a practice that patients choose to visit, not just have to visit.

By implementing these simple changes, you can transform your waiting room from a source of stress and anxiety into a welcoming and comfortable space that enhances the patient experience and makes patients look forward to visiting your clinic.

And it all starts with a mindset shift: a commitment to showing your patients that you genuinely care.

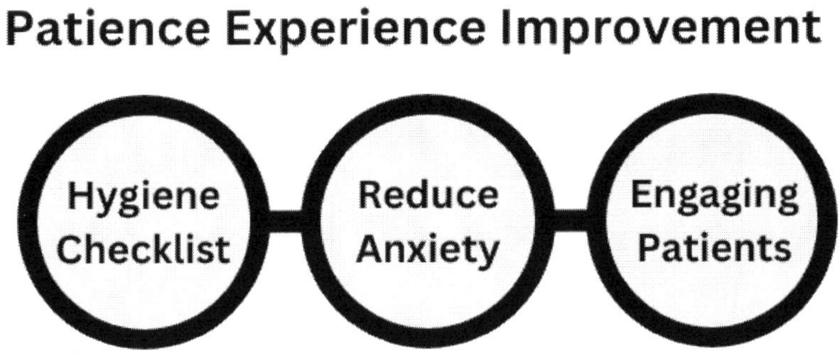

PART 3

COMMUNICATE
THE DOCTOR-PATIENT CONNECTION

Let's be honest, Doctor. In the rush of a busy practice, it's easy to fall into a routine: ask the standard questions, perform the examination, prescribe the medication, and move on. But are you really connecting with your patients? Are you truly understanding their concerns, their fears, and their individual needs?

This section is all about transforming your patient interactions from **transactional to transformational**. It's about building genuine connections that foster trust, improve outcomes, and create a lasting bond between you and your patients.

Active Listening: 3 Questions That Change Everything

> ***"Your stethoscope hears the body. Your silence hears the soul."***

Most doctors hear their patients, but few truly listen. Active listening is more than just nodding; it's about paying full attention, understanding, and responding thoughtfully to what your patients are saying, both verbally and nonverbally. It's about creating a space where they feel heard, valued, and understood.

These three questions are simple, but they can dramatically change the way you interact with your patients:

1. **"How have you really been feeling since I last saw you?"**
   - **Why it works:** This question goes beyond the standard "How are you feeling today?" It encourages patients to reflect on their overall well-being and share any subtle changes they may have noticed.
   - **How to listen:** Pay close attention to their tone of voice, body language, and any hesitation they might have. Don't interrupt or rush them. Let them tell their story in their own words.
2. **"What are your biggest worries about your health right now?"**
   - **Why it works:** This question uncovers the real concerns that are weighing on your patients' minds. It helps you address their anxieties and provide reassurance.
   - **How to listen:** Be empathetic and understanding. Acknowledge their fears and let them know that you're

there to help them. Don't dismiss their concerns, even if they seem irrational.

3. **"Is there anything else you'd like to share with me today?"**
   - **Why it works:** This open-ended question gives patients the opportunity to bring up anything they may have forgotten or were hesitant to mention earlier. It shows that you're willing to listen and address all of their needs.
   - **How to listen:** Be patient and attentive. Sometimes the most important information comes at the very end of the consultation.

Key to Active Listening

- **Pay Attention:** Give the patient your undivided attention. Make eye contact, put away your phone, and minimize distractions.
- **Show That You're Listening:** Use verbal and nonverbal cues to show that you're engaged, such as nodding your head, making eye contact, and saying things like "I see" or "Tell me more."
- **Provide Feedback:** Summarize what the patient has said to ensure you understand correctly. Ask clarifying questions to gather more information.
- **Defer Judgement:** Avoid interrupting or offering unsolicited advice. Let the patient finish speaking even if you already know the solution. Listening fully shows respect.
- **Respond Appropriately:** Offer support, reassurance, and practical advice based on what the patient has shared. Be kind, clear, and solution-focused.

Empathy in Action: Handling Tough Conversations

"Tough conversations become easier when you sit beside, not across."

As a doctor, you're bound to encounter difficult conversations with patients, whether it's delivering bad news, discussing sensitive topics, or addressing their concerns about treatment. In these moments, **empathy** becomes your most powerful tool. It's not just about what you say, but **how** you say it and how your words make your patients **feel**.

What Is Empathy?

Empathy is the ability to understand and share the feelings of another person. It's about putting yourself in your patient's shoes and seeing the situation from their perspective. It doesn't mean you have to agree with them, but it does mean **acknowledging their emotions**, honoring their fears, and showing that **you care**.

Key Phrases for Empathetic Communication

- "I understand this is difficult for you."
- "That sounds incredibly frustrating."
- "I can see that you're worried."
- "It's understandable that you're feeling that way."
- "I'm here to support you through this."

These phrases aren't complicated, but their impact is profound. Use them genuinely and often.

How to Handle Specific Difficult Situations

- **Delivering Bad News:**
  - Be direct and honest, but also compassionate.
  - Use simple language and avoid medical jargon.
  - Allow time and space for the patient to react and express their emotions.
  - Offer hope and support.
  - Provide information about resources and support groups.
- **Discussing Sensitive Topics (e.g., end-of-life care, mental health):**
  - Create a safe and confidential space.
  - Ask open-ended questions and encourage the patient to share their thoughts and feelings.
  - Respect their cultural and religious beliefs.
  - Provide accurate information and dispel any myths or misconceptions.
- **Addressing Patient Concerns about Treatment:**
  - Listen carefully to their concerns and address them with facts and evidence.
  - Explain the risks and benefits of the treatment in a clear and understandable way.
  - Where appropriate, offer alternatives and let them feel involved in the decision.
  - Respect their autonomy, even if their choice goes against your recommendation. Support them regardless.

The Real Power of Empathy

Empathy doesn't just make you a more compassionate doctor; it makes you a **more effective one**. It builds trust, improves compliance, and turns difficult conversations into healing ones.

Building Trust: The Key to Patient Retention

"A doctor's skill treats the illness, but trust treats the patient."

Trust is the cornerstone of the doctor-patient relationship. Without it, even the most advanced treatment plans can fail. When patients trust you, they not only follow your advice more closely but also return to your clinic, refer others, and stay loyal for years.

A trusted doctor becomes more than a medical advisor; they become a partner in the patient's health journey.

How to Build Trust with Your Patients

- **Be Competent:** This is the foundation of trust. Stay up-to-date on the latest medical knowledge and provide high-quality care. Sometimes, just explaining why you're choosing a particular treatment can reinforce your expertise.
- **Be Honest and Transparent:** Be open and honest with your patients about their condition, treatment options, and the potential risks and benefits.
- **Be Reliable and Consistent:** Follow through on your promises and be consistent in your approach to patient care.
- **Be Respectful and Empathetic:** Treat your patients with respect and show that you care about their well-being.
- **Communicate Clearly and Effectively:** Use simple language and avoid medical jargon. Take the time to explain things thoroughly and answer all of their questions.

- **Be Accessible:** Make it easy for patients to contact you or your staff with questions or concerns.
- **Go the Extra Mile:** Show your patients that you care by going above and beyond to meet their needs. This could include calling them after a visit to check on their progress, providing them with helpful resources, or simply offering a listening ear.

The Outcome: A Stronger Bond and a Healthier Practice

By prioritizing communication, empathy, and trust, you can create a doctor-patient connection that will not only improve patient outcomes but also build a thriving and fulfilling practice.

Remember that building a stronger bond will help in retaining your patients, so you can fill your chamber with these proven and helpful methods.

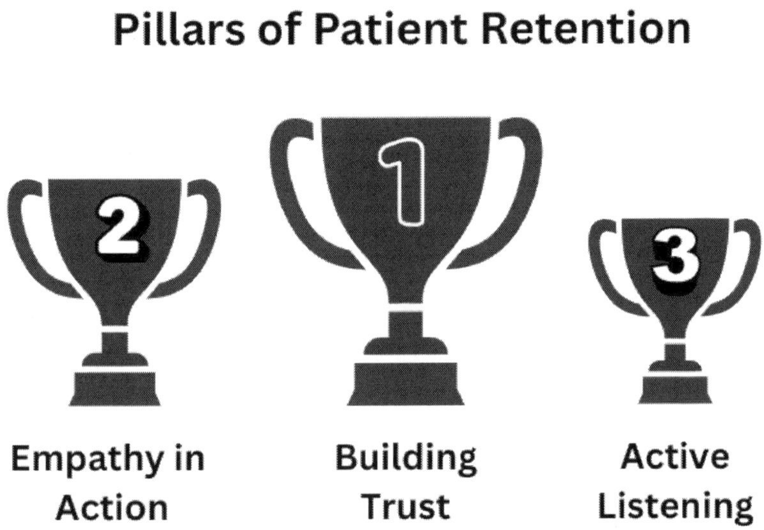

PART 4

EMPOWER

YOUR STAFF, YOUR SECRET WEAPON

Let's face it, Doctor, you can't do it all alone. Every successful practice stands on the shoulders of a dedicated team. Your assistants, receptionists, and support staff are not just handling admin work; they are the *heartbeat* of your clinic. In many ways, they are the face of your practice, the first point of contact for patients, and the key to creating a positive and welcoming atmosphere.

Yet, far too often, these valuable team members are under-trained, under-utilized, and under-appreciated. Doctors don't take time to appreciate their efforts. This is a missed opportunity. When you empower your staff, you are investing in the success of your entire practice. Think of your staff, like a cricket match, you are the captain of the team, and every staff member needs to work together.

Why Staff Training Is Essential

> ***"Clinic ka impression, staff ke expression se banta hai."***

Your assistants are much more than just appointment bookers and receptionists. They are the gatekeepers of your practice, the first impression patients have, and the key to creating a "wow" experience that keeps patients coming back. When your staff is well-trained and empowered, they can:

- **Create a Positive First Impression:** A warm, friendly greeting, a genuine smile, and a helpful attitude can instantly put patients at ease and create a positive first impression.
- **Communicate Effectively in the Local Language:** This is crucial! Your staff must be fluent in the local language (Hindi, Bengali, etc.) to communicate effectively with your patients. This not only builds trust but ensures patients fully understand your instructions, reducing confusion and increasing compliance.
- **Manage the Flow of Patients Effectively:** Trained assistants can efficiently manage appointments, handle phone calls, and ensure that patients are seen in a timely manner, minimizing wait times and reducing frustration.
- **Answer Patient Questions Knowledgeably:** Well-informed staff can answer basic patient questions about appointments, medications, and procedures, saving you valuable time and freeing you up to focus on more complex medical issues.
- **Provide Support and Reassurance:** A caring voice at the reception or someone who notices when a patient looks nervous—these small acts can ease patient anxiety and create a supportive environment.

- **Promote Your Practice Naturally:** Trained assistants can effectively promote your services and build your practice's reputation through positive interactions with patients.

The Importance of Medical Knowledge AND Local Language Proficiency for Your Staff

In addition to basic customer service skills, it's also crucial to equip your staff with a working knowledge of medical terminology, common conditions, and basic treatment protocols. AND they need to be able to communicate all of this in the language your patients understand best.

While they shouldn't be providing medical advice (that's your job!), being able to understand and communicate medical information accurately in the local language can greatly enhance their ability to assist patients.

Here are some areas where medical knowledge and language skills are essential:

- **Understanding Medical Terminology in the Local Language:** Knowing the meaning of common medical terms (and being able to translate them accurately) allows them to understand your instructions and communicate effectively with patients. A staff member who can say "blood pressure" in layman's terms or explain "CBC test" in Hindi makes the patient feel more comfortable.
- **Recognizing Common Symptoms and Describing Them in the Local Language:** Being able to recognize basic symptoms (and ask about them in the patient's language) can help them triage patients and ensure that those with urgent needs are seen promptly.
- **Providing Basic Medication Information in the Local Language:** Knowing the names, dosages, and common

side effects of frequently prescribed medications (and being able to explain them clearly) allows them to answer basic patient questions and provide helpful reminders. For instance: "Ye dawa khane ke baad leni hai"—simple, but so helpful.

- **Educating Patients About Procedures in the Local Language:** Being able to explain common procedures in simple terms (in the local language) can help alleviate patient anxiety and improve compliance.

How to Train Your Staff for Success

Training doesn't have to be complicated or expensive. It just has to be consistent and relevant.

- **Prioritize Local Language Proficiency:** Ensure that all new hires are fluent in the local language. If they are not, provide basic spoken language training to help them communicate better.
- **Invest in Formal Training:** Consider sending your staff to workshops or seminars on customer service, medical terminology, and patient communication (preferably in the local language). These short sessions can significantly improve their confidence and professionalism.
- **Provide Ongoing On-the-Job Training:** Regularly review procedures, provide updates on new medical information, and offer opportunities for staff to practice their skills (in the local language). Even a weekly 20-minute refresher session can go a long way.
- **Encourage Self-Study:** Provide your staff with access to relevant medical textbooks, online resources, and professional journals (in the local language whenever possible). You can even recommend YouTube videos or WhatsApp groups for continuous learning.

- **Lead by Example:** Demonstrate excellent communication skills (in the local language) and a caring attitude in your own interactions with patients. The way you speak, listen, and show empathy becomes the model your team follows.

How to Empower Your Staff to Shine

A good team culture is felt by your patients, too. When your team smiles, your patients smile.

Training is important, but it's not enough. You also need to **empower your staff to take ownership** of their roles and make decisions that benefit your patients and your practice. Empowered staff feel responsible, trusted, and motivated and that shows in the way they serve your patients.

Here's how:

- **Give Them Autonomy:** Allow them to make decisions within their scope of responsibility, such as scheduling appointments, handling phone calls, and resolving minor patient issues.
- **Encourage Initiative:** Encourage them to come up with new ideas and solutions to improve the patient experience.
- **Provide Feedback and Recognition:** Regularly provide feedback on their performance, both positive and constructive. Don't just wait for mistakes, praise them when they handle a difficult patient well or when a patient appreciates their help. A small "thank you" or a monthly "star performer" mention can go a long way in boosting morale.
- **Create a Supportive Work Environment:** Foster a positive and supportive work environment where staff feel valued, respected, and empowered to do their best.

- **Align Them with Your Vision:** Make sure your staff understands your clinic's mission whether it's compassionate care, efficiency, or community outreach. When they know the *why*, they'll deliver more than just tasks, they'll contribute meaningfully to your brand.

When you invest in your staff, **you're investing in the future of your practice**. By providing them with the training, knowledge, and support they need to succeed (including language skills), you can create a team of dedicated professionals who are committed to providing exceptional patient care and building a thriving practice.

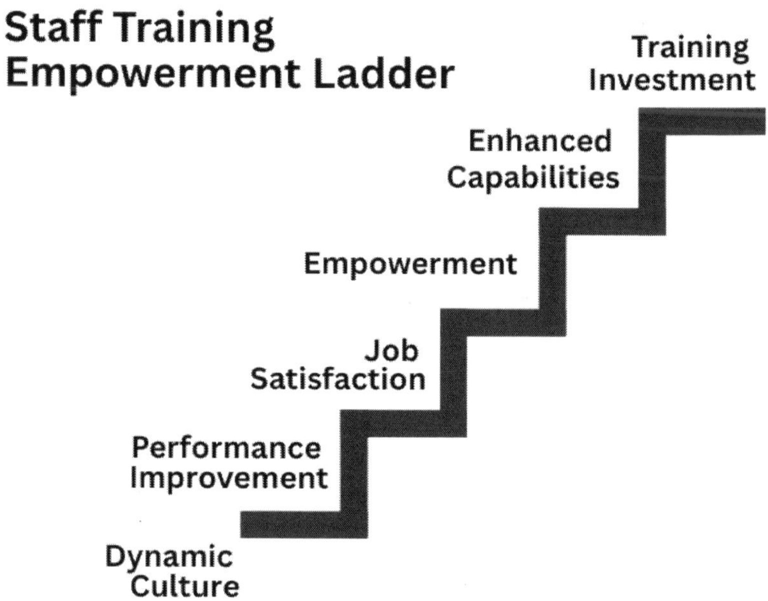

CASE STUDIES
Real Clinics, Real Results

In the next few pages, you'll read about some interesting real-life case studies of doctors who made simple yet smart changes to their practice and saw meaningful results. These examples aren't about fancy tools or big budgets, but about practical steps, better patient experience, and the power of consistency. Whether you're just starting out or have been practicing for years, these stories will give you fresh perspective and inspiration.

CASE STUDY: 1

Dr. Suchismita Roy – General Physician

Dr. Suchismita Roy (Name changed to respect privacy) had been running her small clinic near Barrackpore station for over 12 years. Known for her kind nature and careful diagnosis, she had a loyal but limited set of patients.

When I met her, she said, "Amar chamber ta bhaloi cholche, kintu boro hoye uthchhe na." (My practice is doing okay, but it's not growing.) Her words reflected the quiet frustration many doctors feel when their efforts don't translate into growth. She was relying mostly on word of mouth and wasn't using any patient communication tools. In today's competitive world, that meant staying invisible to many potential patients.

It took me quite some time to convince her, but she finally agreed to start with small changes—sending polite SMS reminders before appointments, a simple "Thank you" in Bengali message after visits, and occasional wellness tips on WhatsApp. These small gestures, though simple, began to create a sense of care even outside the clinic.

We also worked on the waiting area: we added a clean water dispenser, a small hand-sanitising machine, and some Bengali magazines to keep patients engaged. The goal was to turn her clinic into a space that felt warm and welcoming, not just functional. Her staff was also trained to greet patients with a smile and gently collect feedback. A smile, after all, is sometimes the best medicine.

Within just three months, the number of daily patients increased by 20%. Many old patients returned, and new ones came through referrals. Word started spreading, not just about her medical expertise, but about the experience of visiting her clinic.

Dr. Roy said with a smile, "Amar chamber e ekta notun jeebon eshe geche." (It's like my clinic got a new life.)

Case Study: 2

Dr. Arindam Chatterjee – Dental Surgeon

Dr. Arindam Chatterjee (Name changed to respect privacy) runs a dental clinic near Tollygunge. Though he was technically sound and had the latest equipment, he often struggled with patient retention. "Lokera ekbar ashe, abar ashe na... follow-up miss hoye jaye," he told me. (People come once, then don't return... follow-ups get missed.)

His skills weren't in question; it was the **overall experience** that needed attention. We had a detailed discussion on patient experience and trust-building. After all, dentistry is as much about comfort and connection as it is about precision.

First, we introduced a soft instrumental playlist, a diffuser with lavender fragrance, and a screen displaying easy oral care tips. These small sensory touches helped reduce anxiety, which is common among dental patients.

Then we set up an automated SMS system that reminded patients of their next visit and sent a friendly follow-up message after treatment. Just a simple nudge, but it made patients feel remembered and valued. He also recorded a short, warm welcome video that played in the waiting room, making every new visitor feel personally greeted.

Slowly but surely, patients started noticing. They began returning regularly for cleanings, check-ups, and even brought their families. A sense of trust and consistency began to form.

In just four months, his monthly patient count grew by over 25%. Dr. Chatterjee now calls me regularly and keeps coming up with new ideas and now it's me who has to ask him to move slowly!

Case Study 3: Dr. Prabir Sen vs. Dr. Tapas Mitra – Two MBBS Doctors in the Same Colony, Different Outcomes

In a busy residential colony near Dum Dum, Kolkata, two doctors—Dr. Prabir Sen and Dr. Tapas Mitra (Name changed to respect privacy) have been practicing for years. Both hold MBBS degrees, both are well-qualified general physicians, and both opened their chambers around the same time. But over the years, a striking difference has emerged.

Dr. Tapas Mitra charges ₹400 per consultation and keeps things basic. His chamber is often dimly lit, old chairs creak, there's no assistant, and patients are made to wait in silence. He barely looks up while writing prescriptions and rarely follows up unless asked. It's a transactional setup: efficient, perhaps, but emotionally distant.

Just across the street, Dr. Prabir Sen charges ₹950, double the fee but his chamber is a different world. Clean and welcoming, drinking water arranged neatly, and a cheerful assistant at the desk. The moment you walk in, there's a sense of warmth and professionalism. Patients receive SMS reminders, polite thank-you messages post-consultation, and health tips every month, simple yet powerful gestures that show continuity beyond the clinic walls.

He talks to patients with genuine concern, answers their questions calmly, and remembers little details from past visits. That personal touch builds deep trust; something money can't buy. Patients' wait time is minimised and they are given time accordingly. Each visit feels less like a chore and more like care.

Despite the higher fees, Dr. Sen's chamber is always full, often with patients waiting outside. The difference? **Not just the treatment, but the experience**. In today's healthcare landscape, the way you make people feel is just as important as how you treat them.

CONCLUSION

YOUR PATIENT-FIRST PRACTICE: A THRIVING FUTURE

You've reached the end, Doctor! If you've made it this far, I commend you. It shows you're truly dedicated to improving your practice and the lives of your patients. Let me tell you, this isn't just about running a successful business; it's about making a real difference in your community.

It's easy to get caught up in the day-to-day grind, but I want you to remember why you became a doctor in the first place: **to help people, to heal them, and to make their lives better.** By prioritizing your patients and building strong relationships with them, you can achieve that goal while also creating a thriving and fulfilling practice.

The Next Steps: Implementing Your Action Plan

(My Personal Recommendations)

> ***"The clinic that listens, learns, and improves; wins patients for life."***

I know it can seem like a lot to take on at once, so let me share what I'd do if I were in your shoes:

1. **Start with ONE "Keep-In-Touch" Strategy:** Don't try to implement everything at once. Pick the easiest one for you to start. Maybe it's just sending appointment reminders. Then, find someone you trust—a family member, a bright student, or a dependable assistant—to help you automate it. That's what I did, and it was a game-changer.
    - *Keep it simple, and let momentum build from there.*

2. **Make ONE Waiting Room Improvement This Week:** Walk into your waiting room and try to see it through the eyes of a new patient. What's the first thing that jumps out at you? Is it cluttered? Is it too hot? Is it lacking something? Address that one thing this week. Even something small, like adding a few plants, can make a big difference.
    - *Small changes often lead to big impressions.*
3. **Ask Those 3 Key Questions (and Really Listen):** This one takes practice, but it's so worth it. During your next patient consultation, make a conscious effort to ask those three questions: "How have you really been feeling?," "What are your biggest worries?," and "Is there anything else?" Then, truly listen to what they have to say. You'll be amazed at what you learn.
    - *The more you listen, the more they trust you.*
4. **Invest in Your Staff (They're Worth It!):** Think about one skill that would make your staff more effective and confident. Is it better customer service? Is it a better understanding of medical terminology? Send them to a workshop, provide them with some training materials, or simply take the time to teach them yourself. The investment will pay off tenfold. A confident, kind, and capable team becomes your biggest asset.
    - *When your staff grows, your practice grows.*

The Long-Term Payoff: A Practice That's More Than Just a Business (It's a Community)

"When care is real, loyalty is natural."

I know what you're thinking: "This sounds like a lot of work." And it's true, it does take effort. But trust me, the rewards are immeasurable not just in numbers, but in meaning.

By prioritizing patient care and building strong relationships, you'll create a practice that's more than just a business. It'll be a place where:

- **Patients Trust You (and Tell Their Friends!):** That's the best kind of advertising, Doctor. Word-of-mouth is powerful, especially in smaller communities where trust and reputation travel faster than any digital ad.
- **Patients Actually Want to Come Back:** Think about it: how many of your patients dread coming to your office? By creating a welcoming and caring environment, you can change that perception and make your practice a place where patients feel comfortable, understood, and supported.
- **You Feel Fulfilled and Purposeful:** At the end of the day, being a doctor is about more than just making money. It's about making a positive impact on people's lives. When patients come back to say, "I feel better, thanks to you," that's the kind of reward no paycheck can match.
- **You Build a Good Reputation (That Sticks Around):** Reputation isn't built overnight, but it is built in the little things — how your staff answers a call, how clean your clinic feels, or how kindly you explain a diagnosis. Over time, these details shape your image in the community.

So, go ahead, Doctor. Take the leap. Embrace the "patient-first" approach, not as a tactic, but as your core philosophy and watch your practice flourish. I know you can do it!

The Choice is Yours: Stagnate or Thrive?

"If nothing changes, nothing changes. Small steps today bring big shifts tomorrow."

After reading this, after hearing about the simple changes that can deliver such significant results, I know there will be two distinct reactions among the medical community.

1. **The Skeptics: "Nice in Theory, But It Won't Work Here"**

   A segment of doctors will, understandably, dismiss these strategies as impractical, claiming they are suitable for the pages of a book, but not for the realities of their practices. They'll cite their heavy workload, their limited resources, the unique challenges of their location, or the perceived apathy of their patients.

   They might say, *"This is a small village, my patients won't understand marketing,"* or *"I'm too busy to worry about hand sanitizer; I have lives to save."*

   To those doctors, I say: **I respect your perspective. I understand your concerns.** Change is never easy, and old habits die hard. You may be right: these strategies may not work for you.

   But I urge you to consider this: **If you keep doing what you've always done, you'll keep getting what you've always gotten.** And if you're content with that, if the idea of seeing the same number of patients, facing the same struggles, and working with the same stress for the next couple of years sounds acceptable, then perhaps this book isn't for you.

But if even a small part of you believes that *more is possible*: more impact, more connection, more satisfaction then maybe, just maybe, it's worth a try.

2. **The Implementers: "Slowly but Surely, Seeing Real Results"**

   Then there's the other group: the doctors who are willing to try something new, to step outside their comfort zones, and to embrace a more patient-centric approach. These are the doctors who understand that the medical landscape is changing and that adapting to those changes is essential for survival and success.

   They might start small: implementing one "Keep-In-Touch" strategy, making one small improvement to their waiting room, or committing to asking those three key questions during each consultation. They may not see immediate, dramatic results, but they'll stay consistent, they'll monitor their progress, and they'll adjust their approach as needed.

   And, slowly but surely, they'll start to see a difference. They'll notice more patients remembering their appointments. They'll see a more relaxed and engaged atmosphere in their waiting room. They'll hear positive feedback from their patients. And most importantly, they'll start to see their chambers filled with patients, even during the traditionally "off-season" months.

The Choice is Yours

The path you take is entirely up to you. You can continue down the road you've always traveled, clinging to the status quo and hoping for the best...

Or,

You can embrace the changes, implement the strategies outlined in this book, and create a practice that's not only successful but also deeply fulfilling.

I genuinely hope you choose the latter.

Need Help Getting Started? Let's Connect.

If you have any questions, need clarification, or simply want help implementing these ideas in your practice, I'm here for you. You don't have to do it alone.

You can schedule a 1-to-1 meeting with me whether it's to clear your doubts, get personalized guidance, or brainstorm what could work best for your unique setup.

Let's make your patient-first practice a reality, together.

Neerav Shah
Mail Id: theneerav@gmail.com